Exploring the Galaxy

Jupiter

by Thomas K. Adamson

Consulting Editor: Gail Saunders-Smith, Ph.D.

Consultant: James Gerard
Aerospace Education Specialist, NASA
Kennedy Space Center, Florida

Capstone
press

Mankato, Minnesota

Pebble Plus is published by Capstone Press
151 Good Counsel Drive, P.O. Box 669, Mankato, Minnesota 56002
http://www.capstone-press.com

1 2 3 4 5 6 08 07 06 05 04 03

Library of Congress Cataloging-in-Publication Data
Adamson, Thomas K., 1970–
    Jupiter / by Thomas K. Adamson.
    p. cm.—(Pebble Plus: exploring the galaxy)
    Summary: Simple text and photographs describe the planet Jupiter.
    Includes bibliographical references and index.
    ISBN 0-7368-2112-0 (hardcover)
    1. Jupiter (Planet)—Juvenile literature. [1. Jupiter (Planet)] I. Title. II. Series.
QB661 .A33 2004
523.45—dc21   2002155603

Editorial Credits
Mari C. Schuh, editor; Kia Adams, designer; Alta Schaffer, photo researcher; Eric Kudalis, product planning editor

Photo Credits
Digital Vision, 5 (Venus)
John Foster/Photo Researchers, 20-21
NASA, 1, 4 (Pluto), 9, 11, 12-13, 15 (Jupiter), 17, 19; JPL, 5 (Jupiter); JPL/Caltech, 5 (Uranus)
PhotoDisc, Inc., cover, 4 (Neptune), 5 (Earth, Sun, Saturn, Mars, and Mercury), 15 (Earth)
Photri-Microstock/NASA, 6-7

Note to Parents and Teachers

The Exploring the Galaxy series supports national science standards related to earth science. This book describes and illustrates the planet Jupiter. The photographs support early readers in understanding the text. The repetition of words and phrases helps early readers learn new words. This book also introduces early readers to subject-specific vocabulary words, which are defined in the Glossary section. Early readers may need assistance to read some words and to use the Table of Contents, Glossary, Read More, Internet Sites, and Index/Word List sections of the book.

Word Count: 131
Early-Intervention Level: 13

Table of Contents

Jupiter

Jupiter is the fifth planet
from the Sun. Jupiter
is the largest planet
in the solar system.

The Solar System

Jupiter

Sun

Features

Jupiter is made mostly
of gases. It is called
a gas giant.

Jupiter has no solid surface.
A spacecraft cannot land
on Jupiter. But it can study
Jupiter's gases up close.

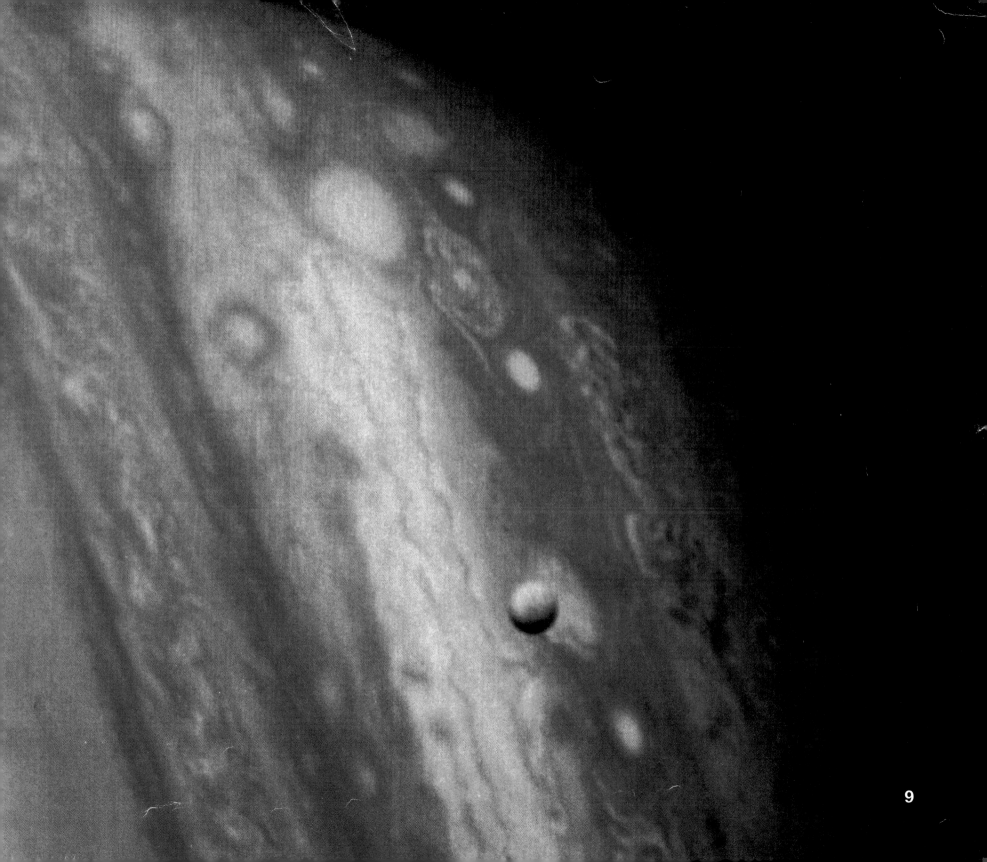

Orange and white clouds
circle Jupiter. The clouds
are thick.

The Great Red Spot is
a large storm on Jupiter.
The storm is twice
as big as Earth.

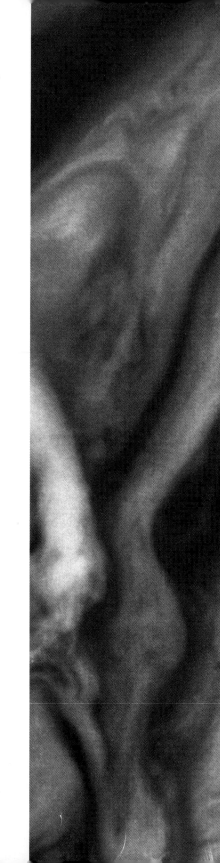

Jupiter's Size

Jupiter is much bigger than Earth. Jupiter is bigger than all of the other planets put together.

Earth

15

Jupiter's Moons

Jupiter has at least
47 moons. Earth has
only one moon.

four of Jupiter's moons

People and Jupiter

People could not breathe

the air on Jupiter. Most

of the air is very thick.

People can see Jupiter
from Earth. Jupiter looks
like a bright star.

Jupiter

Glossary

breathe—to take air in and out of the lungs; people and animals must breathe to live.

gas—a substance, such as air, that spreads to fill any space that holds it; Jupiter is made mostly of gases.

moon—an object that moves around a planet; Io, Europa, Ganymede, and Callisto are Jupiter's largest moons.

planet—a large object that moves around the Sun; Jupiter is the fifth planet from the Sun.

solar system—the Sun and the objects that move around it; our solar system has nine planets and many moons, asteroids, and comets.

spacecraft—a vehicle that travels in space

star—a large ball of burning gases in space

Sun—the star that the planets move around; the Sun provides light and heat for the planets.

Read More

Goss, Tim. *Jupiter.* The Universe. Chicago: Heinemann Library, 2003.

Kerrod, Robin. *Jupiter.* Planet Library. Minneapolis: Lerner, 2000.

Vogt, Gregory L. *Jupiter.* The Galaxy. Mankato, Minn.: Bridgestone Books, 2000.

Internet Sites

Do you want to find out more about Jupiter and the solar system? Let FactHound, our fact-finding hound dog, do the research for you.

Here's how:

1) Visit *http://www.facthound.com*

2) Type in the **Book ID** number: 0736821120

3) Click on **FETCH IT**.

FactHound will fetch Internet sites picked by our editors just for you!

Index/Word List

air, 18

breathe, 18

clouds, 10

Earth, 12, 14, 16, 20

gases, 6, 8

giant, 6

Great Red Spot, 12

moons, 16

orange, 10

people, 18, 20

planet, 4, 14

solar system, 4

solid, 8

spacecraft, 8

star, 20

storm, 12

Sun, 4

surface, 8

thick, 10, 18

white, 10